Drugs Act 2005

CHAPTER 17

Explanatory Notes are available separately

AF719463

GRANGIS UK Publishing

Adapted and published by GRANGIS (Grand Register Library).
Online: www.grangis.com
E-mail: contact@grangis.com

In this version:
ISBN: 979-8-88559-056-3

Note: This is the original version (as it was originally enacted). Title, sub-title and the generated date is as marked on the pages.

Drugs Act 2005

CHAPTER 17

DRUGS ACT 2005

PART 1

SUPPLY OF CONTROLLED DRUGS

PART 2

POLICE POWERS RELATING TO DRUGS

PART 3

ASSESSMENT OF MISUSE OF DRUGS

PART 4

MISCELLANEOUS AND GENERAL

SCHEDULES

Drugs Act 2005

2005 CHAPTER 17

An Act to make provision in connection with controlled drugs and for the making of orders to supplement anti-social behaviour orders in cases where behaviour is affected by drug misuse or other prescribed factors. [7th April 2005]

BE IT ENACTED by the Queen's most Excellent Majesty, by and with the advice and consent of the Lords Spiritual and Temporal, and Commons, in this present Parliament assembled, and by the authority of the same, as follows:—

PART 1

SUPPLY OF CONTROLLED DRUGS

1 Aggravated supply of controlled drug

(1) After section 4 of the Misuse of Drugs Act 1971 (c. 38) (restriction on production and supply of controlled drugs) insert—

"4A Aggravation of offence of supply of controlled drug

(1) This section applies if—

(a) a court is considering the seriousness of an offence under section 4(3) of this Act, and

(b) at the time the offence was committed the offender had attained the age of 18.

(2) If either of the following conditions is met the court—

(a) must treat the fact that the condition is met as an aggravating factor (that is to say, a factor that increases the seriousness of the offence), and

(b) must state in open court that the offence is so aggravated.

(3) The first condition is that the offence was committed on or in the vicinity of school premises at a relevant time.

(4) The second condition is that in connection with the commission of the offence the offender used a courier who, at the time the offence was committed, was under the age of 18.

(5) In subsection (3), a relevant time is—

(a) any time when the school premises are in use by persons under the age of 18;

(b) one hour before the start and one hour after the end of any such time.

(6) For the purposes of subsection (4), a person uses a courier in connection with an offence under section 4(3) of this Act if he causes or permits another person (the courier)—

(a) to deliver a controlled drug to a third person, or

(b) to deliver a drug related consideration to himself or a third person.

(7) For the purposes of subsection (6), a drug related consideration is a consideration of any description which—

(a) is obtained in connection with the supply of a controlled drug, or

(b) is intended to be used in connection with obtaining a controlled drug.

(8) In this section—

"school premises" means land used for the purposes of a school excluding any land occupied solely as a dwelling by a person employed at the school; and

"school" has the same meaning—

(a) in England and Wales, as in section 4 of the Education Act 1996;

(b) in Scotland, as in section 135(1) of the Education (Scotland) Act 1980;

(c) in Northern Ireland, as in Article 2(2) of the Education and Libraries (Northern Ireland) Order 1986."

(2) Section 4A of the Misuse of Drugs Act 1971 (c. 38) (inserted by subsection (1) above) does not apply to an offence committed before this section comes into force.

2 Proof of intention to supply a controlled drug

(1) The Misuse of Drugs Act 1971 is amended as follows.

(2) In section 5 (restriction of possession of controlled drugs), after subsection (4) insert—

"(4A) In any proceedings for an offence under subsection (3) above, if it is proved that the accused had an amount of a controlled drug in his possession which is not less than the prescribed amount, the court or jury must assume that he had the drug in his possession with the intent to supply it as mentioned in subsection (3).

(4B) Subsection (4A) above does not apply if evidence is adduced which is sufficient to raise an issue that the accused may not have had the drug in his possession with that intent.

(4C) Regulations under subsection (4A) above have effect only in relation to proceedings for an offence committed after the regulations come into force."

(3) In section 31 (general provisions as to regulations)—

(a) in subsection (2), after "which shall" insert ", except as provided by subsection (2A),";

(b) after subsection (2) insert—

"(2A) A statutory instrument containing regulations under section 5(4A) of this Act shall not be made unless a draft of the instrument has been laid before, and approved by a resolution of, each House of Parliament.";

(c) after subsection (4) insert—

"(4A) Subsection (4) does not apply in relation to regulations under section 5(4A) of this Act."

(4) In section 38 (special provisions as to Northern Ireland) after subsection (1) insert—

"(1A) Subsection (1) does not apply, in relation to regulations under section 5(4A) of this Act, to the reference to the Secretary of State in the definition of "prescribed" in section 37(1) of this Act."

PART 2

POLICE POWERS RELATING TO DRUGS

3 Drug offence searches: England and Wales

(1) Section 55 of the Police and Criminal Evidence Act 1984 (c. 60) (intimate searches) is amended as follows.

(2) After subsection (3) insert—

"(3A) A drug offence search shall not be carried out unless the appropriate consent has been given in writing.

(3B) Where it is proposed that a drug offence search be carried out, an appropriate officer shall inform the person who is to be subject to it—

(a) of the giving of the authorisation for it; and

(b) of the grounds for giving the authorisation."

(3) After subsection (10) insert—

"(10A) If the intimate search is a drug offence search, the custody record relating to that person shall also state—

(a) the authorisation by virtue of which the search was carried out;

(b) the grounds for giving the authorisation; and

(c) the fact that the appropriate consent was given."

(4) In subsection (11), for "subsection (10)" substitute "subsections (10) and (10A)".

(5) After subsection (13) insert—

"(13A) Where the appropriate consent to a drug offence search of any person was refused without good cause, in any proceedings against that person for an offence—

(a) the court, in determining whether there is a case to answer;

(b) a judge, in deciding whether to grant an application made by the accused under paragraph 2 of Schedule 3 to the Crime and Disorder Act 1998 (applications for dismissal); and

(c) the court or jury, in determining whether that person is guilty of the offence charged,

may draw such inferences from the refusal as appear proper."

(6) In subsection (17) at the appropriate place insert—

"“appropriate officer” means—

(a) a constable,

(b) a person who is designated as a detention officer in pursuance of section 38 of the Police Reform Act 2002 if his designation applies paragraph 33D of Schedule 4 to that Act, or

(c) a person who is designated as a staff custody officer in pursuance of section 38 of that Act if his designation applies paragraph 35C of Schedule 4 to that Act;".

4 Drug offence searches: Northern Ireland

(1) Article 56 of the Police and Criminal Evidence (Northern Ireland) Order 1989 (S.I. 1989/1341) (intimate searches) is amended as follows.

(2) After paragraph (3) insert—

"(3A) A drug offence search shall not be carried out unless the appropriate consent has been given in writing.

(3B) Where it is proposed that a drug offence search be carried out, a constable shall inform the person who is to be subject to it—

(a) of the giving of the authorisation for it; and

(b) of the grounds for giving the authorisation."

(3) After paragraph (10) insert—

"(10A) If the intimate search is a drug offence search, the custody record relating to that person shall also state—

(a) the authorisation by virtue of which the search was carried out;

(b) the grounds for giving the authorisation; and

(c) the fact that the appropriate consent was given."

(4) In paragraph (11), for "paragraph (10)" substitute "paragraphs (10) and (10A)".

(5) After paragraph (13) insert—

"(13A) Where the appropriate consent to a drug offence search of any person was refused without good cause, in any proceedings against that person for an offence—

(a) the court, in determining whether to commit the accused for trial or whether there is a case to answer;

(b) a judge, in deciding whether to grant an application made by the accused under—

(i) Article 5 of the Criminal Justice (Serious Fraud) (Northern Ireland) Order 1988 (application for dismissal of charges where a case of fraud has been transferred from a magistrates' court to the Crown Court under Article 3 of that Order); or

(ii) paragraph 4 of Schedule 1 to the Children's Evidence (Northern Ireland) Order 1995 (application for dismissal of charge of violent or sexual offence involving child in respect of which notice of transfer has been given under Article 4 of that Order); and

(c) the court or jury, in determining whether that person is guilty of the offence charged,

may draw such inferences from the refusal as appear proper."

5 X-rays and ultrasound scans: England and Wales

(1) After section 55 (intimate searches) of the Police and Criminal Evidence Act 1984 (c. 60) insert—

"55A X-rays and ultrasound scans

(1) If an officer of at least the rank of inspector has reasonable grounds for believing that a person who has been arrested for an offence and is in police detention—

(a) may have swallowed a Class A drug, and

(b) was in possession of it with the appropriate criminal intent before his arrest,

the officer may authorise that an x-ray is taken of the person or an ultrasound scan is carried out on the person (or both).

(2) An x-ray must not be taken of a person and an ultrasound scan must not be carried out on him unless the appropriate consent has been given in writing.

(3) If it is proposed that an x-ray is taken or an ultrasound scan is carried out, an appropriate officer must inform the person who is to be subject to it—

(a) of the giving of the authorisation for it, and

(b) of the grounds for giving the authorisation.

(4) An x-ray may be taken or an ultrasound scan carried out only by a suitably qualified person and only at—

(a) a hospital,

(b) a registered medical practitioner's surgery, or

(c) some other place used for medical purposes.

(5) The custody record of the person must also state—

(a) the authorisation by virtue of which the x-ray was taken or the ultrasound scan was carried out,

(b) the grounds for giving the authorisation, and

(c) the fact that the appropriate consent was given.

(6) The information required to be recorded by subsection (5) must be recorded as soon as practicable after the x-ray has been taken or ultrasound scan carried out (as the case may be).

(7) Every annual report—

(a) under section 22 of the Police Act 1996, or

(b) made by the Commissioner of Police of the Metropolis,

must contain information about x-rays which have been taken and ultrasound scans which have been carried out under this section in the area to which the report relates during the period to which it relates.

(8) The information about such x-rays and ultrasound scans must be presented separately and must include—

(a) the total number of x-rays;

(b) the total number of ultrasound scans;

(c) the results of the x-rays;

(d) the results of the ultrasound scans.

(9) If the appropriate consent to an x-ray or ultrasound scan of any person is refused without good cause, in any proceedings against that person for an offence—

(a) the court, in determining whether there is a case to answer,

(b) a judge, in deciding whether to grant an application made by the accused under paragraph 2 of Schedule 3 to the Crime and Disorder Act 1998 (applications for dismissal), and

(c) the court or jury, in determining whether that person is guilty of the offence charged,

may draw such inferences from the refusal as appear proper.

(10) In this section "the appropriate criminal intent", "appropriate officer", "Class A drug" and "suitably qualified person" have the same meanings as in section 55 above."

(2) In Schedule 4 to the Police Reform Act 2002 (c. 30)—

(a) after paragraph 33C (inserted by paragraph 7 of Schedule 9 to the Serious Organised Crime and Police Act 2005 (c. 15)) insert—

"33D Where a designation applies this paragraph to any person, he is authorised to carry out the duty under—

(a) section 55 of the Police and Criminal Evidence Act 1984 of informing a person who is to be subject to an intimate search under that section of the matters of which he is required to be informed in pursuance of subsection (3B) of that section;

(b) section 55A of that Act of informing a person who is to be subject to x-ray or ultrasound (as the case may be) under that section of the matters of which he is required to be informed in pursuance of subsection (3) of that section.";

(b) after paragraph 35B (inserted by paragraph 10 of Schedule 9 to the Serious Organised Crime and Police Act 2005) insert—

"35C Where a designation applies this paragraph to any person, he is authorised to carry out the duty under—

(a) section 55 of the Police and Criminal Evidence Act 1984 of informing a person who is to be subject to an intimate search under that section of the matters of which he is required to be informed in pursuance of subsection (3B) of that section;

(b) section 55A of that Act of informing a person who is to be subject to x-ray or ultrasound (as the case may be) under that section of the matters of which he is required to be informed in pursuance of subsection (3) of that section."

6 X-rays and ultrasound scans: Northern Ireland

After Article 56 (intimate searches) of the Police and Criminal Evidence (Northern Ireland) Order 1989 (S.I. 1989/1341) insert—

"56A X-rays and ultrasound scans

(1) If an officer of at least the rank of superintendent has reasonable grounds for believing that a person who has been arrested for an offence and is in police detention—

(a) may have swallowed a Class A drug, and

(b) was in possession of it with the appropriate criminal intent before his arrest,

the officer may authorise that an x-ray is taken of the person or an ultrasound scan is carried out on the person (or both).

(2) An x-ray must not be taken of a person and an ultrasound scan must not be carried out on him unless the appropriate consent has been given in writing.

(3) If it is proposed that an x-ray is taken or an ultrasound scan is carried out, a constable must inform the person who is to be subject to it—

(a) of the giving of the authorisation for it, and

(b) of the grounds for giving the authorisation.

(4) An x-ray may be taken or an ultrasound scan carried out only by a suitably qualified person and only at—

(a) a hospital,

(b) a registered medical practitioner's surgery, or

(c) some other place used for medical purposes.

(5) The custody record of the person must also state—

(a) the authorisation by virtue of which the x-ray was taken or the ultrasound scan was carried out,

(b) the grounds for giving the authorisation, and

(c) the fact that the appropriate consent was given.

(6) The information required to be recorded by subsection (5) must be recorded as soon as practicable after the x-ray has been taken or ultrasound scan carried out (as the case may be).

(7) Every annual report under section 58 of the Police (Northern Ireland) Act 2000 must contain information about x-rays which have been taken and ultrasound scans which have been carried out under this Article during the period to which it relates.

(8) The information about such x-rays and ultrasound scans must be presented separately and must include—

(a) the total number of x-rays;

(b) the total number of ultrasound scans;

(c) the results of the x-rays;

(d) the results of the ultrasound scans.

(9) If the appropriate consent to an x-ray or ultrasound scan of any person is refused without good cause, in any proceedings against that person for an offence—

(a) the court, in determining whether to commit the accused for trial or whether there is a case to answer,

(b) a judge, in deciding whether to grant an application made by the accused under—

(i) Article 5 of the Criminal Justice (Serious Fraud) (Northern Ireland) Order 1988 (application for dismissal of charges where a case of fraud has been transferred from a magistrates' court to the Crown Court under Article 3 of that Order), or

(ii) paragraph 4 of Schedule 1 to the Children's Evidence (Northern Ireland) Order 1995 (application for dismissal of charge of violent or sexual offence involving child in respect of which notice of transfer has been given under Article 4 of that Order), and

(c) the court or jury, in determining whether that person is guilty of the offence charged,

may draw such inferences from the refusal as appear proper.

(10) In this Article "the appropriate criminal intent", "Class A drug" and "suitably qualified person" have the same meanings as in Article 56 above."

7 Testing for presence of Class A drugs

(1) Section 63B of the Police and Criminal Evidence Act 1984 (c. 60) ("PACE") (testing for presence of Class A drugs) is amended in accordance with subsections (2) to (12).

(2) In subsection (1) for "the following conditions are met" substitute "—

(a) either the arrest condition or the charge condition is met;

(b) both the age condition and the request condition are met; and

(c) the notification condition is met in relation to the arrest condition, the charge condition or the age condition (as the case may be)."

(3) After subsection (1) insert—

"(1A) The arrest condition is that the person concerned has been arrested for an offence but has not been charged with that offence and either—

(a) the offence is a trigger offence; or

(b) a police officer of at least the rank of inspector has reasonable grounds for suspecting that the misuse by that person of a specified Class A drug caused or contributed to the offence and has authorised the sample to be taken."

(4) In subsection (2), for "The first condition is" substitute "The charge condition is either".

(5) For subsection (3) substitute—

"(3) The age condition is—

(a) if the arrest condition is met, that the person concerned has attained the age of 18;

(b) if the charge condition is met, that he has attained the age of 14."

(6) In subsection (4), for "third" substitute "request".

(7) After subsection (4) insert—

"(4A) The notification condition is that—

(a) the relevant chief officer has been notified by the Secretary of State that appropriate arrangements have been made for the police area as a whole, or for the particular police station, in which the person is in police detention, and

(b) the notice has not been withdrawn.

(4B) For the purposes of subsection (4A) above, appropriate arrangements are arrangements for the taking of samples under this section from whichever of the following is specified in the notification—

(a) persons in respect of whom the arrest condition is met;

(b) persons in respect of whom the charge condition is met;

(c) persons who have not attained the age of 18."

(8) In subsection (5)(b) after "subsection" insert "(1A)(b) or".

(9) After subsection (5A) insert—

"(5B) If a sample is taken under this section from a person in respect of whom the arrest condition is met no other sample may be taken from him under this section during the same continuous period of detention but—

(a) if the charge condition is also met in respect of him at any time during that period, the sample must be treated as a sample taken by virtue of the fact that the charge condition is met;

(b) the fact that the sample is to be so treated must be recorded in the person's custody record.

(5C) Despite subsection (1)(a) above, a sample may be taken from a person under this section if—

(a) he was arrested for an offence (the first offence),

(b) the arrest condition is met but the charge condition is not met,

(c) before a sample is taken by virtue of subsection (1) above he would (but for his arrest as mentioned in paragraph (d) below) be required to be released from police detention,

(d) he continues to be in police detention by virtue of his having been arrested for an offence not falling within subsection (1A) above, and

(e) the sample is taken before the end of the period of 24 hours starting with the time when his detention by virtue of his arrest for the first offence began.

(5D) A sample must not be taken from a person under this section if he is detained in a police station unless he has been brought before the custody officer."

(10) For subsection (6A) substitute—

"(6A) The Secretary of State may by order made by statutory instrument amend—

(a) paragraph (a) of subsection (3) above, by substituting for the age for the time being specified a different age specified in the order, or different ages so specified for different police areas so specified;

(b) paragraph (b) of that subsection, by substituting for the age for the time being specified a different age specified in the order."

(11) In subsection (7), after paragraph (a) insert—

"(aa) for the purpose of informing any decision about the giving of a conditional caution under Part 3 of the Criminal Justice Act 2003 to the person concerned;".

(12) Subsection (9) is omitted.

(13) On the day this section comes into force the notification condition must be treated as being met—

(a) for the purposes of the charge condition in relation to a police area, if subsection (2) of section 63B of PACE is in force immediately before that day in relation to the police area;

(b) for the purposes of the age condition in relation to a police area or police station, if before that day notification was given under subsection (9) of that section in relation to the police area or police station and was not withdrawn,

and "age condition", "charge condition" and "notification condition" have the same meaning as in section 63B of PACE (as amended by this section).

(14) Subsection (13) above does not prevent the Secretary of State withdrawing a notification which is treated as made by virtue of that subsection.

8 Extended detention of suspected drug offenders

In section 152 of the Criminal Justice Act 1988 (c. 33) (remand of suspected drug offenders)—

(a) in the title leave out "customs";

(b) after subsection (1) insert—

"(1A) In subsection (1) the power of a magistrates' court to remand a person to customs detention for a period not exceeding 192 hours includes power to commit the person to the custody of a constable to be detained for such a period."

PART 3

ASSESSMENT OF MISUSE OF DRUGS

9 Initial assessment following testing for presence of Class A drugs

(1) This section applies if—

(a) a sample is taken under section 63B of PACE (testing for presence of Class A drug) from a person detained at a police station,

(b) an analysis of the sample reveals that a specified Class A drug may be present in the person's body,

(c) the age condition is met, and

(d) the notification condition is met.

(2) A police officer may, at any time before the person is released from detention at the police station, require him to attend an initial assessment and remain for its duration.

(3) An initial assessment is an appointment with a suitably qualified person (an "initial assessor")—

(a) for the purpose of establishing whether the person is dependent upon or has a propensity to misuse any specified Class A drug,

(b) if the initial assessor thinks that he has such a dependency or propensity, for the purpose of establishing whether he might benefit from further assessment, or from assistance or treatment (or both), in connection with the dependency or propensity, and

(c) if the initial assessor thinks that he might benefit from such assistance or treatment (or both), for the purpose of providing him with advice, including an explanation of the types of assistance or treatment (or both) which are available.

(4) The age condition is met if the person has attained the age of 18 or such different age as the Secretary of State may by order made by statutory instrument specify for the purposes of this section.

(5) In relation to a person ("A") who has attained the age of 18, the notification condition is met if—

(a) the relevant chief officer has been notified by the Secretary of State that arrangements for conducting initial assessments for persons who have attained the age of 18 have been made for persons from whom samples have been taken (under section 63B of PACE) at the police station in which A is detained, and

(b) the notice has not been withdrawn.

(6) In relation to a person ("C") who is of an age which is less than 18, the notification condition is met if—

(a) the relevant chief officer has been notified by the Secretary of State that arrangements for conducting initial assessments for persons of that age have been made for persons from whom samples have been taken (under section 63B of PACE) at the police station in which C is detained, and

(b) the notice has not been withdrawn.

(7) In subsections (5) and (6), "relevant chief officer" means the chief officer of police of the police force for the police area in which the police station is situated.

10 Follow-up assessment

(1) This section applies if—

(a) a police officer requires a person to attend an initial assessment and remain for its duration under section 9(2),

(b) the age condition is met, and

(c) the notification condition is met.

(2) The police officer must, at the same time as he imposes the requirement under section 9(2)—

(a) require the person to attend a follow-up assessment and remain for its duration, and

(b) inform him that the requirement ceases to have effect if he is informed at the initial assessment that he is no longer required to attend the follow-up assessment.

(3) A follow-up assessment is an appointment with a suitably qualified person (a "follow-up assessor")—

(a) for any of the purposes of the initial assessment which were not fulfilled at the initial assessment, and

(b) if the follow-up assessor thinks it appropriate, for the purpose of drawing up a care plan.

(4) A care plan is a plan which sets out the nature of the assistance or treatment (or both) which may be most appropriate for the person in connection with any dependency upon, or any propensity to misuse, a specified Class A drug which the follow-up assessor thinks that he has.

(5) The age condition is met if the person has attained the age of 18 or such different age as the Secretary of State may by order made by statutory instrument specify for the purposes of this section.

(6) In relation to a person ("A") who has attained the age of 18, the notification condition is met if—

(a) the relevant chief officer has been notified by the Secretary of State that arrangements for conducting follow-up assessments for persons who have attained the age of 18 have been made for persons from whom samples have been taken (under section 63B of PACE) at the police station in which A is detained, and

(b) the notice has not been withdrawn.

(7) In relation to a person ("C") who is of an age which is less than 18, the notification condition is met if—

(a) the relevant chief officer has been notified by the Secretary of State that arrangements for conducting follow-up assessments for persons of that age have been made for persons from whom samples have been taken (under section 63B of PACE) at the police station in which C is detained, and

(b) the notice has not been withdrawn.

(8) In subsections (6) and (7), "relevant chief officer" means the chief officer of police of the police force for the police area in which the police station is situated.

11 Requirements under sections 9 and 10: supplemental

(1) This section applies if a person is required to attend an initial assessment and remain for its duration by virtue of section 9(2).

(2) A police officer must—

(a) inform the person of the time when, and the place at which, the initial assessment is to take place, and

(b) explain that this information will be confirmed in writing.

(3) A police officer must warn the person that he may be liable to prosecution if he fails without good cause to attend the initial assessment and remain for its duration.

(4) If the person is also required to attend a follow-up assessment and remain for its duration by virtue of section 10(2), a police officer must also warn the person that he may be liable to prosecution if he fails without good cause to attend the follow-up assessment and remain for its duration.

(5) A police officer must give the person notice in writing which—

(a) confirms that he is required to attend and remain for the duration of an initial assessment or both an initial assessment and a follow-up assessment (as the case may be),

(b) confirms the information given in pursuance of subsection (2), and

(c) repeats the warning given in pursuance of subsection (3) and any warning given in pursuance of subsection (4).

(6) The duties imposed by subsections (2) to (5) must be discharged before the person is released from detention at the police station.

(7) A record must be made, as part of the person's custody record, of—

(a) the requirement imposed on him by virtue of section 9(2),

(b) any requirement imposed on him by virtue of section 10(2),

(c) the information and explanation given to him in pursuance of subsection (2) above,

(d) the warning given to him in pursuance of subsection (3) above and any warning given to him in pursuance of subsection (4) above, and

(e) the notice given to him in pursuance of subsection (5) above.

(8) If a person is given a notice in pursuance of subsection (5), a police officer or a suitably qualified person may give the person a further notice in writing which—

(a) informs the person of any change to the time when, or to the place at which, the initial assessment is to take place, and

(b) repeats the warning given in pursuance of subsection (3) and any warning given in pursuance of subsection (4).

12 Attendance at initial assessment

(1) This section applies if a person is required to attend an initial assessment and remain for its duration by virtue of section 9(2).

(2) The initial assessor must inform a police officer or a police support officer if the person—

(a) fails to attend the initial assessment at the specified time and place, or

(b) attends the assessment at the specified time and place but fails to remain for its duration.

(3) A person is guilty of an offence if without good cause—

(a) he fails to attend an initial assessment at the specified time and place, or

(b) he attends the assessment at the specified time and place but fails to remain for its duration.

(4) A person who is guilty of an offence under subsection (3) is liable on summary conviction to imprisonment for a term not exceeding 51 weeks, or to a fine not exceeding level 4 on the standard scale, or to both.

(5) If a person fails to attend an initial assessment at the specified time and place, any requirement imposed on him by virtue of section 10(2) ceases to have effect.

(6) In this section—

(a) the specified time, in relation to the person concerned, is the time specified in the notice given to him in pursuance of subsection (5) of section 11 or, if a further notice specifying a different time has been given to him in pursuance of subsection (8) of that section, the time specified in that notice, and

(b) the specified place, in relation to the person concerned, is the place specified in the notice given to him in pursuance of subsection (5) of section 11 or, if a further notice specifying a different place has been given to him in pursuance of subsection (8) of that section, the place specified in that notice.

(7) In relation to an offence committed before the commencement of section 281(5) of the Criminal Justice Act 2003 (c. 44) (alteration of penalties for summary offences), the reference in subsection (4) to 51 weeks is to be read as a reference to 3 months.

13 Arrangements for follow-up assessment

(1) This section applies if—

(a) a person attends an initial assessment in pursuance of section 9(2), and

(b) he is required to attend a follow-up assessment and remain for its duration by virtue of section 10(2).

(2) If the initial assessor thinks that a follow-up assessment is not appropriate, he must inform the person concerned that he is no longer required to attend the follow-up assessment.

(3) The requirement imposed by virtue of section 10(2) ceases to have effect if the person is informed as mentioned in subsection (2).

(4) If the initial assessor thinks that a follow-up assessment is appropriate, the assessor must—

(a) inform the person of the time when, and the place at which, the follow-up assessment is to take place, and

(b) explain that this information will be confirmed in writing.

(5) The assessor must also warn the person that, if he fails without good cause to attend the follow-up assessment and remain for its duration, he may be liable to prosecution.

(6) The initial assessor must also give the person notice in writing which—

(a) confirms that he is required to attend and remain for the duration of the follow-up assessment,
(b) confirms the information given in pursuance of subsection (4), and
(c) repeats the warning given in pursuance of subsection (5).

(7) The duties mentioned in subsections (2) and (4) to (6) must be discharged before the conclusion of the initial assessment.

(8) If a person is given a notice in pursuance of subsection (6), the initial assessor or another suitably qualified person may give the person a further notice in writing which—
(a) informs the person of any change to the time when, or to the place at which, the follow-up assessment is to take place, and
(b) repeats the warning mentioned in subsection (5).

14 Attendance at follow-up assessment

(1) This section applies if a person is required to attend a follow-up assessment and remain for its duration by virtue of section 10(2).

(2) The follow-up assessor must inform a police officer or a police support officer if the person—
(a) fails to attend the follow-up assessment at the specified time and place, or
(b) attends the assessment at the specified time and place but fails to remain for its duration.

(3) A person is guilty of an offence if without good cause—
(a) he fails to attend a follow-up assessment at the specified time and place, or
(b) he attends the assessment at the specified time and place but fails to remain for its duration.

(4) A person who is guilty of an offence under subsection (3) is liable on summary conviction to imprisonment for a term not exceeding 51 weeks, or to a fine not exceeding level 4 on the standard scale, or to both.

(5) In this section—
(a) the specified time, in relation to the person concerned, is the time specified in the notice given to him in pursuance of subsection (6) of section 13 or, if a further notice specifying a different time has been given to him in pursuance of subsection (8) of that section, the time specified in that notice, and
(b) the specified place, in relation to the person concerned, is the place specified in the notice given to him in pursuance of subsection (6) of section 13 or, if a further notice specifying a different place has been given to him in pursuance of subsection (8) of that section, the place specified in that notice.

(6) In relation to an offence committed before the commencement of section 281(5) of the Criminal Justice Act 2003 (c. 44) (alteration of penalties for summary offences), the reference in subsection (4) to 51 weeks is to be read as a reference to 3 months.

15 Disclosure of information about assessments

(1) An initial assessor may disclose information obtained as a result of an initial assessment to any of the following—

(a) a person who is involved in the conduct of the assessment;

(b) a person who is or may be involved in the conduct of any follow-up assessment.

(2) A follow-up assessor may disclose information obtained as a result of a follow-up assessment to a person who is involved in the conduct of the assessment.

(3) Subject to subsections (1) and (2), information obtained as a result of an initial or a follow-up assessment may not be disclosed by any person without the written consent of the person to whom the assessment relates.

(4) Nothing in this section affects the operation of section 17(4).

16 Samples submitted for further analysis

(1) A requirement imposed on a person by virtue of section 9(2) or 10(2) ceases to have effect if at any time before he has fully complied with the requirement—

(a) a police officer makes arrangements for a further analysis of the sample taken from him as mentioned in section 9(1)(a), and

(b) the analysis does not reveal that a specified Class A drug was present in the person's body.

(2) If a requirement ceases to have effect by virtue of subsection (1), a police officer must so inform the person concerned.

(3) Nothing in subsection (1) affects the validity of anything done in connection with the requirement before it ceases to have effect.

(4) If a person fails to attend an assessment which he is required to attend by virtue of section 9(2) or fails to remain for the duration of such an assessment but, at any time after his failure, the requirement ceases to have effect by virtue of subsection (1) above—

(a) no proceedings for an offence under section 12(3) may be brought against him, and

(b) if any such proceedings were commenced before the requirement ceased to have effect, those proceedings must be discontinued.

(5) If a person fails to attend an assessment which he is required to attend by virtue of section 10(2) or fails to remain for the duration of such an assessment but, at any time after his failure, the requirement ceases to have effect by virtue of subsection (1) above—

(a) no proceedings for an offence under section 14(3) may be brought against him, and

(b) if any such proceedings were commenced before the requirement ceased to have effect, those proceedings must be discontinued.

17 Relationship with Bail Act 1976 etc.

(1) A requirement imposed on a person by virtue of section 9(2) or 10(2) ceases to have effect if at any time before he has fully complied with the requirement—

(a) he is charged with the related offence, and

(b) a court imposes on him a condition of bail under section 3(6D) of the Bail Act 1976 (c. 63) (duty to impose condition to undergo relevant assessment etc.).

(2) For the purposes of section 3(6D) of the 1976 Act, a relevant assessment (within the meaning of that Act) is to be treated as having been carried out if—

(a) a person attends an initial assessment and remains for its duration, and

(b) the initial assessor is satisfied that the initial assessment fulfilled the purposes of a relevant assessment.

(3) For the purposes of paragraph 6B(2)(b) of Schedule 1 to the 1976 Act (exceptions to right to bail for drug users in certain areas), a person is to be treated as having undergone a relevant assessment (within the meaning of that Act) if—

(a) the person attends an initial assessment and remains for its duration, and

(b) the initial assessor is satisfied that the initial assessment fulfilled the purposes of a relevant assessment.

(4) An initial assessor may disclose information relating to an initial assessment for the purpose of enabling a court considering an application for bail by the person concerned to determine whether subsection (2) or (3) applies.

(5) Nothing in subsection (1) affects—

(a) the validity of anything done in connection with the requirement before it ceases to have effect, or

(b) any liability which the person may have for an offence under section 12(3) or 14(3) committed before the requirement ceases to have effect.

(6) In subsection (1), "the related offence" is the offence in respect of which the condition specified in subsection (1A) or (2) of section 63B of PACE is satisfied in relation to the taking of the sample mentioned in section 9(1)(a) of this Act.

18 Orders under this Part and guidance

(1) A statutory instrument containing an order under section 9(4) or 10(5) must not be made unless a draft of the instrument has been laid before, and approved by a resolution of, each House of Parliament.

(2) Any such order may—

(a) make different provision for different police areas;

(b) make such provision as the Secretary of State considers appropriate in connection with requiring persons who have not attained the age of 18 to attend and remain for the duration of an initial assessment or a follow-up assessment (as the case may be), including provision amending this Part.

(3) In exercising any functions conferred by this Part, a police officer and a suitably qualified person must have regard to any guidance issued by the Secretary of State for the purposes of this Part.

19 Interpretation

(1) This section applies for the purposes of this Part.

(2) "Class A drug" and "misuse" have the same meanings as in the Misuse of Drugs Act 1971 (c. 38).

(3) "Specified", in relation to a Class A drug, has the same meaning as in Part 3 of the Criminal Justice and Court Services Act 2000 (c. 43).

(4) "Initial assessment" and "initial assessor" must be construed in accordance with section 9(3).

(5) "Follow-up assessment" and "follow-up assessor" must be construed in accordance with section 10(3).

(6) "Suitably qualified person" means a person who has such qualifications or experience as are from time to time specified by the Secretary of State for the purposes of this Part.

(7) "Police support officer" means a person who is employed by a police authority under section 15(1) of the Police Act 1996 (c. 16) and who is under the direction and control of the chief officer of police of the police force maintained by that authority.

(8) "PACE" means the Police and Criminal Evidence Act 1984 (c. 60).

PART 4

MISCELLANEOUS AND GENERAL

20 Anti-social behaviour orders: intervention orders

(1) After section 1F of the Crime and Disorder Act 1998 (c. 37) (inserted by section 142(1) of the Serious Organised Crime and Police Act 2005 (c. 15)) insert—

"**1G Intervention orders**

(1) This section applies if, in relation to a person who has attained the age of 18, a relevant authority—

(a) makes an application for an anti-social behaviour order or an order under section 1B above (the behaviour order),

(b) has obtained from an appropriately qualified person a report relating to the effect on the person's behaviour of the misuse of controlled drugs or of such other factors as the Secretary of State by order prescribes, and

(c) has engaged in consultation with such persons as the Secretary of State by order prescribes for the purpose of ascertaining that, if the report recommends that an order under this section is made, appropriate activities will be available.

(2) The relevant authority may make an application to the court which is considering the application for the behaviour order for an order under this section (an intervention order).

(3) If the court—

(a) makes the behaviour order, and

(b) is satisfied that the relevant conditions are met,

it may also make an intervention order.

(4) The relevant conditions are—

(a) that an intervention order is desirable in the interests of preventing a repetition of the behaviour which led to the behaviour order being made (trigger behaviour);

(b) that appropriate activities relating to the trigger behaviour or its cause are available for the defendant;

(c) that the defendant is not (at the time the intervention order is made) subject to another intervention order or to any other treatment relating to the trigger behaviour or its cause (whether on a voluntary basis or by virtue of a requirement imposed in pursuance of any enactment);

(d) that the court has been notified by the Secretary of State that arrangements for implementing intervention orders are available in the area in which it appears that the defendant resides or will reside and the notice has not been withdrawn.

(5) An intervention order is an order which—

(a) requires the defendant to comply, for a period not exceeding six months, with such requirements as are specified in the order, and

(b) requires the defendant to comply with any directions given by a person authorised to do so under the order with a view to the implementation of the requirements under paragraph (a) above.

(6) An intervention order or directions given under the order may require the defendant—

(a) to participate in the activities specified in the requirement or directions at a time or times so specified;

(b) to present himself to a person or persons so specified at a time or times so specified.

(7) Requirements included in, or directions given under, an intervention order must, as far as practicable, be such as to avoid—

(a) any conflict with the defendant's religious beliefs, and

(b) any interference with the times (if any) at which he normally works or attends an educational establishment.

(8) If the defendant fails to comply with a requirement included in or a direction given under an intervention order, the person responsible for the provision or supervision of appropriate activities under the order must inform the relevant authority of that fact.

(9) The person responsible for the provision or supervision of appropriate activities is a person of such description as is prescribed by order made by the Secretary of State.

(10) In this section—

"appropriate activities" means such activities, or activities of such a description, as are prescribed by order made by the Secretary of State for the purposes of this section;

"appropriately qualified person" means a person who has such qualifications or experience as the Secretary of State by order prescribes;

"controlled drug" has the same meaning as in the Misuse of Drugs Act 1971;

"relevant authority" means a relevant authority for the purposes of section 1 above.

(11) An order under this section made by the Secretary of State may make different provision for different purposes.

(12) This section and section 1H below apply to a person in respect of whom a behaviour order has been made subject to the following modifications—

(a) in subsection (1) above paragraph (a) must be ignored;

(b) in subsection (2) above, for "is considering the application for" substitute "made";

(c) in subsection (3) above paragraph (a), the word "and" following it and the word "also" must be ignored.

1H Intervention orders: explanation, breach, amendment etc.

(1) Before making an intervention order the court must explain to the defendant in ordinary language—

(a) the effect of the order and of the requirements proposed to be included in it,

(b) the consequences which may follow (under subsection (3) below) if he fails to comply with any of those requirements, and

(c) that the court has power (under subsection (5) below) to review the order on the application either of the defendant or of the relevant authority.

(2) The power of the Secretary of State under section 174(4) of the Criminal Justice Act 2003 includes power by order to—

(a) prescribe cases in which subsection (1) does not apply, and

(b) prescribe cases in which the explanation referred to in that subsection may be made in the absence of the defendant, or may be provided in written form.

(3) If a person in respect of whom an intervention order is made fails without reasonable excuse to comply with any requirement included in the order he is guilty of an offence and liable on summary conviction to a fine not exceeding level 4 on the standard scale.

(4) If the behaviour order as a result of which an intervention order is made ceases to have effect, the intervention order (if it has not previously ceased to have effect) ceases to have effect when the behaviour order does.

(5) On an application made by—

(a) a person subject to an intervention order, or

(b) the relevant authority,

the court which made the intervention order may vary or discharge it by a further order.

(6) An application under subsection (5) made to a magistrates' court must be made by complaint.

(7) If the behaviour order as a result of which an intervention order was made is varied, the court varying the behaviour order may by a further order vary or discharge the intervention order.

(8) Expressions used in this section and in section 1G have the same meaning in this section as in that section."

(2) In section 114(2) of that Act (procedure for subordinate legislation) after "1A" insert ", 1G".

21 Inclusion of mushrooms containing psilocin etc. as Class A drugs

In Part 1 of Schedule 2 to the Misuse of Drugs Act 1971 (c. 38) (Class A drugs), in paragraph 1, insert at the appropriate place—

"Fungus (of any kind) which contains psilocin or an ester of psilocin."

22 Financial provision

There shall be paid out of money provided by Parliament—

(a) any expenditure incurred by the Secretary of State by virtue of this Act, and

(b) any increase attributable to this Act in the sums payable out of money so provided under any other Act.

23 Amendments and repeals

(1) Schedule 1 (which contains amendments) has effect.

(2) Schedule 2 (which contains repeals) has effect.

24 Short title, commencement and extent

(1) This Act may be cited as the Drugs Act 2005.

(2) This section and section 22 come into force on the day on which this Act is passed.

(3) Otherwise, this Act comes into force on such day as the Secretary of State may by order made by statutory instrument appoint.

(4) Different days may be appointed for different purposes.

(5) An order under subsection (3) may make—

(a) any supplementary, incidental or consequential provision, and

(b) any transitory, transitional or saving provision,

as the Secretary of State considers necessary or expedient in connection with the order.

(6) Subject to subsection (7), this Act (except this section and sections 22 and 23) extends to England and Wales only.

(7) So far as it amends or repeals any enactment, this Act has the same extent as the enactment amended or repealed.

SCHEDULES

SCHEDULE 1

Section 23

AMENDMENTS

Police and Criminal Evidence Act 1984 (c. 60)

1 The Police and Criminal Evidence Act 1984 is amended as follows.

2 In section 37 (duties of custody officer before charge), after subsection (8) insert—

"(8A) Subsection (8B) applies if the offence for which the person is arrested is one in relation to which a sample could be taken under section 63B below and the custody officer—

(a) is required in pursuance of subsection (2) above to release the person arrested and decides to release him on bail, or

(b) decides in pursuance of subsection (7)(a) or (b) above to release the person without charge and on bail.

(8B) The detention of the person may be continued to enable a sample to be taken under section 63B, but this subsection does not permit a person to be detained for a period of more than 24 hours after the relevant time."

3 In section 38 (duties of custody officer after charge)—

(a) in subsection (1)(a) for sub-paragraph (iiia) substitute—

"(iiia) in a case where a sample may be taken from the person under section 63B below, the custody officer has reasonable grounds for believing that the detention of the person is necessary to enable the sample to be taken from him;";

(b) in subsection (6A), in the definition of "minimum age" for "section 63B(3) below" substitute "section 63B(3)(b) below".

4 In section 63B(7) (purposes for which results of drug tests may be disclosed), after paragraph (c) insert—

"(ca) for the purpose of an assessment which the person concerned is required to attend by virtue of section 9(2) or 10(2) of the Drugs Act 2005;

(cb) for the purpose of proceedings against the person concerned for an offence under section 12(3) or 14(3) of that Act;".

Criminal Justice and Court Services Act 2000 (c. 43)

5 In section 57 of the Criminal Justice and Court Services Act 2000, subsection (5) (power of Secretary of State to extend section 63B of the Police and Criminal Evidence Act 1984 (c. 60) to persons arrested but not charged) is omitted.

Criminal Justice and Police Act 2001 (c. 16)

6 Section 38 of the Criminal Justice and Police Act 2001 (which amends section 8 of the Misuse of Drugs Act 1971 (c. 38) to create an offence of permitting the use of a controlled drug on premises) is omitted.

Anti-social Behaviour Act 2003 (c. 38)

7 In section 1 of the Anti-social Behaviour Act 2003 (closure notices) after subsection (7) insert—

> "(7A) For the purpose of subsection (6)(a) a constable may enter any premises to which this section applies, using reasonable force if necessary."

Criminal Justice Act 2003 (c. 44)

8 In section 5 of the Criminal Justice Act 2003 (drug testing for under-eighteens), subsection (3)(a) is omitted.

SCHEDULE 2

Section 23

REPEALS

Short title and chapter	*Extent of repeal*
Police and Criminal Evidence Act 1984 (c. 60)	Section 63B(9)
Criminal Justice and Court Services Act 2000 (c. 43)	Section 57(5)
Criminal Justice and Police Act 2001 (c. 16)	Section 38
Criminal Justice Act 2003 (c. 44)	In section 5(3), paragraph (a)

Adapted and published by GRANGIS under the OGL Licence 3.0.

www.nationalarchives.gov.uk/doc/open-government-licence/version/3/

GRANGIS - UK PUBLISHING 2022.

Thank you for taking the time to leave us a review regarding this version

★★★★★

For further inquiries, contact us at:
www.grangis.com / contact@grangis.com

www.ingramcontent.com/pod-product-compliance
Lightning Source LLC
LaVergne TN
LVHW060214210926
848481LV00008B/2742
* 9 7 9 8 8 8 5 5 9 0 5 6 3 *